La Tierra en acción/Earth in Action

Volcanes/Volcanoes

por/by Mari Schuh

Editora consultora/Consulting Editor: Gail Saunders-Smith, PhD

Consultora/Consultant: Susan L. Cutter, PhD
Distinguida Profesora y Directora de Carolina/Carolina Distinguished Professor and Director
Instituto de Investigación de Peligros y Vulnerabilidad/Hazards & Vulnerability Research Institute
Departamento de Geografía/Department of Geography
University of South Carolina

CAPSTONE PRESS
a capstone imprint

Pebble Plus is published by Capstone Press,
151 Good Counsel Drive, P.O. Box 669, Mankato, Minnesota 56002.
www.capstonepub.com

 Books published by Capstone Press are manufactured with paper
containing at least 10 percent post-consumer waste.

Library of Congress Cataloging-in-Publication Data
Schuh, Mari C., 1975–
    [Volcanoes. Spanish & English]
    Volcanes = Volcanoes / por Mari Schuh.
    p. cm.—(Pebble Plus bilingüe. La tierra en acción = Pebble Plus bilingual. Earth in action)
    Summary: "Describes volcanoes, how they form, and the damage they cause—in both English and Spanish"—
Provided by publisher.
    Includes index.
    ISBN 978-1-4296-5357-2 (library binding)
    1. Volcanoes—Juvenile literature. I. Title. II. Title: Volcanoes. III. Series.
QE521.3.S37918 2011
551.21—dc22   2010004994

Editorial Credits
Erika L. Shores, editor; Strictly Spanish, translation services; Lori Bye, set designer; Wanda Winch, media researcher;
    Eric Manske and Danielle Ceminsky, designers; Laura Manthe, production specialist

Photo Credits
Art Life Images/age fotostock/Worldscapes, 21
Capstone Press/Anne P. McMullen, 9, 11
DigitalVision (Getty Images), 13
Getty Images Inc./National Geographic/Carsten Peter, cover
James P. Rowan, 17
Peter Arnold Inc./Weatherstock, 5
Photodisc, 15
Shutterstock/Dmitry Pichugin, 19; Hiroshi Ichikawa, 1; Tatyana Morozova (Manamana), 7

Note to Parents and Teachers

The La Tierra en acción/Earth in Action set supports national science standards related to earth
science. This book describes and illustrates volcanoes in both English and Spanish. The images
support early readers in understanding the text. The repetition of words and phrases helps early
readers learn new words. This book also introduces early readers to subject-specific vocabulary
words, which are defined in the Glossary section. Early readers may need assistance to read
some words and to use the Table of Contents, Glossary, Internet Sites, and Index sections of
the book.

Printed in the United States of America in North Mankato, Minnesota.
112010   006003R

Table of Contents

Tabla de contenidos

What Is a Volcano?

Volcanoes are openings

in the earth's surface.

They let hot lava, rocks,

gas, and ash into the air.

¿Qué es un volcán?

Los volcanes son aberturas en

la superficie de la Tierra. Ellos

permiten que lava caliente, rocas,

gases y cenizas entren al aire.

Some volcanoes look like mountains.

Others are flat and low.

Some volcanoes are
under the ocean.

Algunos volcanes parecen montañas.

Otros son planos y bajos.

Algunos volcanes están
bajo el océano.

Where Volcanoes Form

Most volcanoes form near the edges
of continents. Many volcanoes make
up the Ring of Fire. This area is in the
Pacific Ocean.

Dónde se forman los volcanes

La mayoría de los volcanes se forma cerca
de los bordes de los continentes. Muchos
volcanes forman el Anillo de Fuego.
Esta área está en el Océano Pacífico.

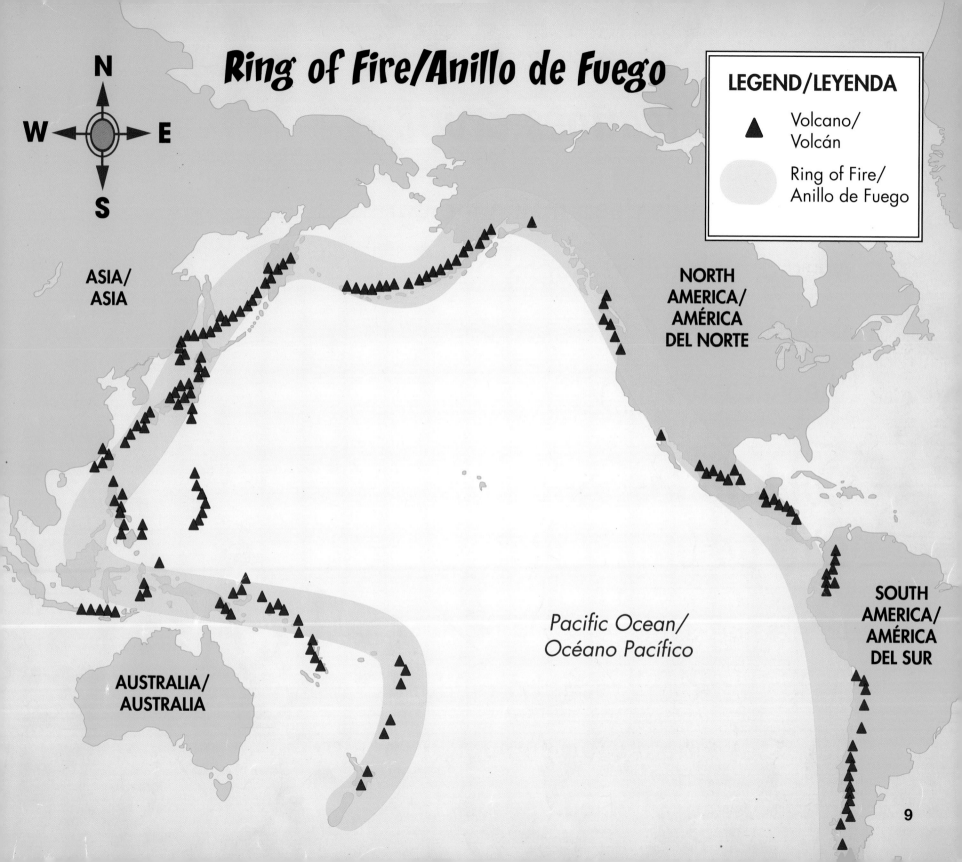

Ring of Fire/Anillo de Fuego

N W E S

LEGEND/LEYENDA

▲ Volcano/ Volcán

◯ Ring of Fire/ Anillo de Fuego

ASIA/ ASIA

NORTH AMERICA/ AMÉRICA DEL NORTE

Pacific Ocean/ Océano Pacífico

AUSTRALIA/ AUSTRALIA

SOUTH AMERICA/ AMÉRICA DEL SUR

9

When Volcanoes Erupt

Pressure builds deep inside the earth.

Melted rock called magma

is pushed toward the surface.

The volcano erupts.

Cuando los volcanes entran en erupción

La presión aumenta en la profundidad

de la Tierra. Las rocas derretidas

llamadas magma son empujadas hacia

la superficie. El volcán erupciona.

Surface/Superficie

Magma/Magma

When magma reaches
the surface, it's called lava.

Lava flows down the volcano.

It covers nearby plants, houses,

and streets.

Cuando el magma llega a la superficie
se llama lava. La lava sale del volcán.

Ella cubre plantas, casas y

calles cercanas.

Ash and dust fill the air.
The ash and dust cover
everything for miles
around the volcano.

Ceniza y polvo llenan el aire.
La ceniza y el polvo cubren todo
por millas alrededor del volcán.

Later, life returns to the area.

Plants and crops

begin to grow again.

Más adelante, la vida vuelve

al área. Las plantas y los cultivos

comienzan a crecer nuevamente.

Studying Volcanoes

Scientists watch volcanoes

and measure their activity.

They collect and study

ash and lava.

Estudiar los volcanes

Los científicos observan volcanes

y miden su actividad.

Ellos recolectan y estudian

las cenizas y la lava.

Scientists try to predict

when a volcano will erupt.

People can be warned to leave

the area to stay safe.

Los científicos tratan de predecir

cuándo entrará en erupción un volcán.

La gente puede ser advertida para que

deje el área y permanezca segura.

Glossary

ash—a powder that results from an explosion; ash comes out of a volcano when it erupts

continent—one of Earth's seven large land masses

erupt—to burst out suddenly with great force

lava—the hot, liquid rock that pours out of a volcano when it erupts

magma—melted rock that is found beneath the earth; after magma breaks through Earth's surface, it is called lava

pressure—the force produced by pressing on something

Ring of Fire—a line of volcanoes that circles around the Pacific Ocean; the Ring of Fire is sometimes called the Pacific Ring of Fire

Internet Sites

FactHound offers a safe, fun way to find Internet sites related to this book. All of the sites on FactHound have been researched by our staff.

Here's all you do:

Visit *www.facthound.com*

Type in this code: 9781429653572

Glosario

el Anillo de Fuego—una línea de volcanes que forma un círculo alrededor del Océano Pacífico; al Anillo de Fuego se lo llama a veces Anillo de Fuego del Pacífico

la ceniza—polvo que resulta de una explosión; la ceniza sale de un volcán cuando erupciona

el continente—uno de los siete cuerpos del suelo de la Tierra

erupcionar—explotar repentinamente con mucha fuerza

la lava—roca caliente y líquida que se derrama desde un volcán cuando erupciona

el magma—roca derretida que se encuentra en el interior de la Tierra; después que el magma sale de la superficie de la Tierra, se llama lava

la presión—la fuerza producida al presionar algo

Sitios de Internet

FactHound brinda una forma segura y divertida de encontrar sitios de Internet relacionados con este libro. Todos los sitios en FactHound han sido investigados por nuestro personal.

Esto es todo lo que tienes que hacer:

Visita *www.facthound.com*

Ingresa este código: 9781429653572

Index

Índice